Trembling

Trembling

Poems by

Karen Petersen

© 2023 Karen Petersen. All rights reserved.
This material may not be reproduced in any form, published,
reprinted, recorded, performed, broadcast,
rewritten or redistributed without
the explicit permission of Karen Petersen.
All such actions are strictly prohibited by law.

Cover design by Karen Petersen

ISBN: 978-1-63980-398-9

Kelsay Books
502 South 1040 East, A-119
American Fork, Utah 84003
Kelsaybooks.com

"Armed with grit and tenderness,
Karen Petersen writes with the fluid mastery of a maestro.
Trembling reads with keen brilliance;
and is both visceral and cerebral."

—Kelvin Kellman,
Editor in Chief, *The Stockholm Review of Literature*

Acknowledgments

Thank you to the previous publications, where versions of these poems previously appeared:

The 5-2: Poems on Crime: "The Last Battle"

A New Ulster: "Emergency"

The Lineup: Poems on Crime: "Baghdad Memories"

New Mexico Poetry Anthology: "Elemental"

Snakeskin: "Morning Minuet"

Where Are You From? A Bilingual Anthology in English and Persian: "Baby"

Prizes:

"Emergency" was nominated for a Pushcart Prize and for The Forward Prize (UK)

"The Last Battle" was nominated for Best of the Net

Trembling won The Wil Mills 2022 Chapbook Award which falls under the auspice of the Iris N. Spencer Poetry Awards that were created by Kean W. Spencer in honor of his mother, a reader and community servant. The Wil Mills Award is open to poets who have published chapbooks but have no full-length collections. Manuscripts are submitted to the West Chester University Poetry Center for judging.

Special thanks to the Poetry Center at West Chester University for sponsoring the Prize and to Judge Annie Finch.

Contents

Trembling	13
The North	14
Obscurité	15
Emergency	16
The Unbearable Lightness of Time	17
Baby	18
Singing	19
PTSD	20
A February Hour	21
Baghdad Memories	22
Morning Minuet	23
Gone	24
A Local Suicide	25
Faster Than a Speeding Bullet	26
Terra	27
The Return	28
Small Signs	30
Leaving Long Island	31
The Last Battle	32
Love	33
Elemental	34
2020	35
Heart	36

She was feeling, thinking, trembling about everything; agitated, happy, miserable, infinitely obliged, absolutely angry.
—Jane Austen

Trembling

All beings tremble.
Fear. Passion. Anticipation.
A deer, sensing the hunter.
You, feeling my touch.
A cat, while being stroked.
The delicate shaking.
The message of living.
The message of dying.
The world is trembling.

The North

How can I begin to tell you of my hunger,
this yearning for the world of silence?
"Ah-HAH" I give the Sami command for "Go"
and the sled runners begin to fly
over low hill after frozen river after . . .
and all the land gives itself to me,
surrounds me.
The wind rushes everywhere,
the sled packing the snow
with a hard, dry crunch, wet spray of slush,
shoosh and sway, the Huskies' labored breathing
the only sound, as the cold,
impartial and deadly, descends.
The sound of death waits in my breath,
but still I love this land,
its slow unfolding beauty.
I glory in the smallness of things,
the vastness of things,
the harshness and the rapture.
"OO-Ya" I give the command for "Stop"
and bury my face in the lead dog's fur,
to feel his warmth, the wildness of his life.
I celebrate the sound of his beating heart.

Obscurité

It's deep night, I'm restless, lost
among the many bed sheets,
pillows, duvet, and oblivious cats.
The dog, twitching and barking in her dreams,
is suddenly awake, alert, *couchant,*
hearing something real outside.
Then her tail begins to wag;
the night wanderers have gone now,
and the house is back asleep, released.

Emergency

Skyrocketing blood pressure, weakening veins,
confused thinking, massive headache, trembling,
a semi-coherent call to 911.
Is this just a run-through, or will it be the end?
I see the seriousness on the EMT's face,
although too delirious now to be frightened
I surrender to the rocking of the ambulance, my cradle,
its lights flashing red through the blinding snow.
Of course that December night it was a blizzard,
the ambulance struggling through the side streets
like a drowning animal trying to survive,
me chattering mindlessly all the while
unaware of the precipice.

Black ice everywhere, white-out conditions,
the driver moving our small, fragile world forward
almost by instinct on the vanished road.
Suddenly there is the hospital,
a bunkered, sacred fortress on the hill,
the castle of my salvation, surrounded by white,
bright light everywhere. I wonder: is this the light
of death, or is this the light of my redemption?
It bears down on me, laser-like, and then there it is:
EMERGENCY, in blood red letters, someone rushing over,
saying "you are going to be okay," dissolving me into tears,
as I know now I have held onto my precious life
only by a state of grace.

The Unbearable Lightness of Time

She likes the art upon her walls.
Their stories do not change.
The Autumn apples falling,
the lone Chinese monk
wandering the hills;
bystanders in her solitude.

These reminders of a life
are her company of multitudes.
Her memories, good
and bad, fade away with time,
and what's left is oblivion,
shredding her like a knife.

Baby

Enjoy the delirious delicious newborn days
soft face luminous in the dark, small feet kicking
my darling what eyes you have, and oh
your little hands grasping for the world:
You are pure love, my sweet love,
and as the sunrise of each day begins
your life awaits you like an opening rose.

Singing

The soul sings a measured gaiety
(within you, I am)
Has no care for propriety
(I am here, and everywhere my love)

Unmeasured, she rises from the dust
Unmeasured, she returns

The heart carries us
(we are all chosen)
But those who turn away—
will find no sanctuary.

PTSD

Breaking out
in a cold sweat
from 30,000 feet,
I imagine
bodies falling
through torn skies.
The air
is a benevolent
blue, the earth
hard and distinct.

I jump
at the unheard,
heart racing,
while others
do the crossword
and doze.
I cannot control
an engine stalling,
pitching us
down into
the wheat fields
of Kansas.

Outside is a
quivering red
horizon as we begin
landing;
rubber on concrete,
engines screaming.
Then heartbeat slowing,
plane on the ground:
the bearable truth.

A February Hour

The birds are dancing in the sky today,
a welcome prologue to Spring.
Soon, the fickle weather of the heart
will arrive, windswept and fraught,
ready to wander through landscapes
of promise and folly.
But today is cloudless, a robin's egg blue,
a vision of grace for a simple soul,
rebuilding love, moment by moment,
the lightning strike on the far horizon
irrelevant, the melting ground
opening to the world again.

Baghdad Memories

The girl just stood there, patiently,
little hand grasping a white purse
that was small like her.
Her other hand rested on a stand
holding a profusion of paper flowers,
her fingertips
touching the edge of a red poppy,
just so.
But it was her eyes,
haunted and dark,
the solemn set of her mouth
that got my attention.
This is all that's left of my childhood,
she seemed to say:
a purse, some shoes,
a lacy embroidered dress.
I waited for an adult to come
and claim her, but nobody came.
As I drove by later
past the shuttered ironwork
of abandoned shops and cratered streets,
the sky at sunset
was as red as that poppy
And she was still there, waiting,
little white shoes facing forward.

Morning Minuet

In memory of Theodore Roethke

How often the office gossips
make life miserable
(as if it isn't fluorescent enough already)

Clock faces, envelopes, swivel chairs
Don't you feel the way those lights look

Who'd live that way
folded into a desk file, neatly put aside
I like sharp pencils—

Your teasing eyes scare me.

Gone

I was in a hall that had no door
no windows I could see
and then the hall became so small
there wasn't room for me
so I lost a life and no one knew
that I'd been this way before
Once I had a door to open
and now there's nothing more.

A Local Suicide

It began with the whispers.
Gary won't be here for a while.
The adults refused to say why.

Suddenly, at lunch, the whole school knew.
The news spreading like a poison in the air.
Gary's father had killed himself.

With a shotgun.
That morning, around 8 a.m.
He put on a suit, then blew his brains out.

After school, the bus passed the small house.
Empty. Abandoned. Darkness.
There is the house of death, I thought.

Blood on the linoleum.
Brains on the fridge.
In another room, a woman screaming.

At least that's how I imagined it.

Faster Than a Speeding Bullet

And He flew up to Heaven's blue, blue skies
so fast even Superman didn't see Him
or the weather satellite or CNN
This Messiah's too hot to handle
yes Sir, no messin' with Him
Calling all sinners
the Ghost in the machine is a-comin'
and then we'll all get some.

Terra

a found poem, for Clifton Wiens

There was an opening in the Earth.
So I made a mark, and then another.
Some days the lines were straight.
Other days were circles.
Always imperfections.
You cannot rake when it's too wet,
and you cannot rake when it's too dry.
I try to accept the imperfections.

The Return

This was the year I lost my voice.
Words, sentences, language
used to flow out of me like a magician
pulling from his mouth long strings of pearls.
Then the string broke.
Oh, I could talk all right,
but it was my inner voice
that had slipped away slowly
like a boat leaving its moorings
and gently drifting out to sea.

At the hospital
I thought I was the odd one out.
Something in me had collapsed
but I had two arms and two legs,
these other people were in wheelchairs.
And then there she was,
a young pretty girl, injured
but all smiles,
greeting a man also in a wheelchair,
seeing only him.

As she leaned forward,
the gown slipped off her thin shoulders.
Her skin was the palest pink,
like a rare Galician rose.
A deep line, angry red,
wound its snakelike way down her spine,
but she was oblivious to my stare.
Although one leg and half an arm
was all that remained on her torso
hers was the attitude of a toreador,
fierce and proud in her loving.

Suddenly I felt small, petty,
silly for having gawked.
I had to admire her defiance,
dwelling in that arcade of
needles, muscle, metal, pain.
Then she was swallowed by an elevator
and vanished,
smiling and talking
as if it were that easy.
I never saw her again.

As the nurse puts a hot towel on my neck
it's like a warm embrace,
the only warmth in my life now.
How pitiful I think, and then
my anger forces me to remember
remember the half-woman, all-woman,
and the love on her face,
the world she has made for herself.
Holding that inside me, I know I am not lost.

Small Signs

No longer winter, not yet spring
in the forest sits a small bird
singing the song of a thousand desires.
The bird's longing fills the silence
waiting for an answer:
I will, I will.

Slowly now you take my hand
and bring it to your lips.

Leaving Long Island

The 5:57 hurtles past fields of darkness
its mournful whistle-cry heard only by
tom cats on the prowl in the dare of night.
I'm seduced, and want to leap off the train
run toward the small lights of slumbering towns,
the twinkling connection
of separate lives and a little peace.
But drunks and babies fast asleep
are all that's left of innocence.
The sky is now yellow, the darkness electric
The city is coming, no one knows anyone there.

The Last Battle

I used to know the names of all the birds
it was more than just words,
I felt their melodies in my soul
but now the land rises up like a fist
and we have all grown old.

The helicopter comes and we run
we run, like deer towards life
while behind there are eyes
that see only frayed cots
and death's warm rot.

And then he died, quietly,
wrapped in a blanket of gold foil
like some small sacrificial offering
to a cruel god
and we all cried-he was only five.

I used to know the songs of all the birds
but it's been so long since I heard
even the simplest one:
gone is the moon, gone is the sun,
we are all undone.

Love

There is a place
where the moon meets the earth
and the grass meets the sky
and where you
and where I
sang a song of the night.
I do not know
what tomorrow will bring
but remember always
that you are loved.

Elemental

Went out briefly under dark afternoon skies
to the edge of the arroyo sliding away
into the rest of the wandering world.
Checked the mail, called in the dog,
breathed the fresh air as the thunder rumbled
and the rain threatened heavily.
All coming down now
lighting striking the far horizon
and the fierce wet wall almost blinding me.
Crept back to the house with the barking dog
whipped by tree boughs, slippery rivulets,
shifting earth, I'm bent over, circumflexed,
put in my place by Nature.

2020

You've only just remembered
all the friends who are now gone
and the sunsets left to gaze upon,
the sighing wind,
the velvet fur of purring cats
and the clinging breath
you still have lying in that bed
as others nearby pass on.
You hear the counting clock,
the tiny baby's cry,
and feel the crumbling shell of life,
so fragile.

Heart

It's about the blood and the guts
and the passion,
visceral,
opening up ourselves
we find our god in our dreams;
in giving our selves away
to the sea at its deepest place
we must always begin, although we
live in a world that's always ending,
remember to do it with heart.

About the Author

Karen Petersen has published short stories, flash, and poetry both nationally and internationally in a variety of publications. In 2019, she was the first person in the history of the Pushcart Prize to receive five nominations in three categories: poetry, short story, and flash. In 2021, two of her poems were nominated for the UK's Forward Prize and the Best of the Net, and in 2022, a poem was long-listed for Australia's international Peter Porter Prize. Her poems have been translated into Persian and Spanish.

More information can be found at:
karenpetersenwriter.com